During the days of Moses, Joshua stood as one of his close helpers.

Moses went up Mount Sinai listen to God and receive the Ten Commandments. Joshua followed Moses halfway up the mountain, and waited for him to return.

Joshua grew close to God as he worked with Moses to lead the people of Israel.

Joshua, his buddy Caleb, and 10 other spies went to the promised land of Canaan to see how the people of Israel could move in.

Joshua and Caleb came back with good news, even good food. But the 10 other spies came back in fear. So the people of Israel doubted God's promise and had to wait many years.

When Moses got old and died, Joshua became the next leader.
"Be strong and of good courage!" God told Joshua.

Joshua was a good leader: humble enough to ask for help and wise enough to make good decisions.

It was time for people of Israel to make their way to the land that God had promised.

"Take down your tents and pack up your things. We will go and cross the Jordan river into the promised land of Canaan." Joshua told the people.

But there was a problem. The Jordan river was huge, and they had no boats. They had no bridge. How would they get across?

"Carry the Ark of the Covenant into the middle of the river!" Joshua told the priests. As soon as the feet of the priests touched the water, the river stopped flowing and dried up.

All the people of Israel safely crossed to the other side, on dry ground.

Then Joshua and a few men piled heavy rocks in the middle of the river bed, as a reminder of God's miracle.

As soon as the priests stepped out of the river with the Ark of the Covenant, the water began to flow again. Isn't that amazing?

The people of Israel set up camp on the other side of the Jordan river. Joshua had led them to the new land that God had promised.

But there were other people not far away, who lived in cities. The biggest city was Jericho. It was surrounded by thick heavy walls.

God told Joshua "The city of Jericho is in the land that I promised for you, so it must go! Follow My instructions carefully."

Joshua obeyed God's message and told the men to march around Jericho. They did so for 6 days.

On the seventh day they marched around seven times. That was a lot of marching. But no one talked, swung a sword or threw a spear.

Joshua could have thought. "What a crazy idea. I have a better plan."
But no! Joshua obeyed God in the smallest of details.

At the end of their last march, Joshua said "Priests, blow your trumpets, people shout as loud as you can and make all the noise you want!"

The walls of the city began to shake, the bricks began to crumble...

...and the great walls came tumbling to the ground. Wham!

It's amazing what God can do for someone who has courage and faith to obey God. Now the people of Israel could live in their beautiful promised land.

Published by iCharacter Ltd. (Ireland)
www.icharacter.org
By Agnes and Salem de Bezenac
Illustrated by Agnes de Bezenac
Copyright 2015. All rights reserved.

Copyright © 2015 by iCharacter Ltd.. All rights reserved. No part of this book may be reproduced in any form or by any electronic or mechanical means, including information storage and retrieval systems, without written permission from the publisher or author, except in the case of a reviewer, who may quote brief passages embodied in critical articles or in a review.

www.ingramcontent.com/pod-product-compliance
Lightning Source LLC
Chambersburg PA
CBHW081503070526
44586CB00019B/2467